INDEX

Joining the Unit

I was almost the first person in my family to join the armed forces and that too getting commissioned in the Indian Army as an officer. There were many things that were unlearnt and many more that were learnt at the Indian Military Academy. I had got commissioned in the Madras regiment. On commissioning we had a short break of 21 days annual leave after which I had to go to our Regimental Center which was at Wellington near Ooty in Tamilnadu, for a period of two weeks.

There was excitement at having got commissioned as an Army Officer and there was curiosity as to how life would be as an officer. At the Regimental center we were given an introduction to the Regimental History and the Regimental Language which was Tamil. Learning these two things were very important as I was going to be in the Madras Regiment for life.

My unit was in Kapurthala and I had to go to Kapurthala from Wellington. This was quite a complicated journey as there were no direct trains. There was one train from Conoor to Delhi and a second from Delhi to Jalandhar. From Jalandhar there was a meter gauge for which no reservations could be made. I was carrying one trunk and one hold-all.

I had written demi official letters to the commanding officer and the Adjutant, but I had not been able to convey the exact ETA (expected time of arrival) to them. I reached the unit gate in a cycle rickshaw, kept my luggage at the RP gate and walked into the Adjutants office with my moment order. He asked me how come I had come without informing him about my ETA. He then called another who was the junior most officer till the time I reported and who was my senior subaltern. He came and stood there as he asked him as to how I had come without informing him, and why he had not groomed me. He had a peculiar style of being bossy. I was surprised as this was the first time I was meeting him. Lt . My senior was an Ex NDA with one year service in the unit. He cast one glance at me and understood that I was the new second lieutenant who was to join the unit. He stood there with a serious disposition while I was standing there and smiling. The Adjutant admonished me for smiling (with a typical Army style ' wipe that smile off your face and shove it up your ***). Within the next 5 minutes there were three more officers who had come into the Adjutants office and were shooting questions at me. I was finding it difficult to control my smile and it was not customary for a youngster to be smiling in front of the seniors, when they were on a ragging spree, and definitely not from a young subaltern who had just joined the unit.

I was interviewed by the Commanding Officer and the Second in Command. Both conveyed their best wishes on joining the unit and urged me to do well.

The initial ragging and grooming was a part of the customs and traditions of the unit and other things I was supposed to stay in the unit lines for about one week. I also took it in my stride. But staying with the Jawans was important as I came to know their interpersonal behavior, habits and customs. On the third day I was told to move back to the Offrs Mess. There was a small cosy room which was allotted to me and I was happy. It seemed like being granted bail for good conduct.

Our Subedar Major was a gallantry award winner, a Maha Vir Chakra from 71 war. Our unit had got a battle Honour of 'Battle of Basantar' and he had earned his Maha Vir Chakra in these Ops. I looked up to him with lot of respect. In a short while he informed me that the next day Bravo company was having BPET and that I was supposed to be running with them. Of course these orders were from the Adjutant. This was painful.

Till the time I joined the Indian Military Academy, I was a tea totaller. This was barring one instance when I attended a party with some retired Army personnel after I had cleared my services selection board interview. At the Indian Military Academy when I was in my first term I was running errands for some of my senior cadets, the third termers, which included getting cigarettes for one of them. Then one day for some reason I was depressed. Something big had happened in my life for which I could not do anything as I could not leave the training and go back to resolve the issues. I went to purchase a packet of cigarettes for my senior and I purchased one packet for myself. That night I smoked ten cigarettes. That was enough to make me a regular smoker. I regretted it but I was not able to stop it. When I went to the regimental center after commissioning I had heard that in the units it was customary to wine in an officer who had newly joined the unit. This was other than the official Dining in. The officers' mess in the Regimental Center had a wonderful bar and the bar NCO was good at making cocktails. Besides it was not difficult to find company of some officer who was regular at the bar. So there I started drinking. All this had added lethargy to me and made me weak, but come what may I had to run BPET (5 km with pack 08 and weapon). And I had to come in some respectable enclosure. I decided to have light dinner and sleep early. But at 1930 hrs in the evening my senior officers were there in the mess to wine me in. So here I was drinking peg after peg and eating snacks and joking nonsence. My senior subaltern had quietly vanished from the mess as he did not approve of this.

Anyway, I ran the next morning and managed to come in satisfactory. My senior was in excellent. But I was just happy the BPET was over.

 On the fifth day, I was called to the office by the Adjutant and handed over an invitation card for my 'Dinning In' into the officers mess.

Notes :

 Dinning In of an officer is a regular custom in the Indian Army. The officers who are dined in are supposed to be the guests and there are drinks and good food. And the Dinner is followed by a speech by the commanding officer, welcoming the officer to the unit. This is followed by a speech by the officer who has been 'Dined In'.

Going to places in trains is as it is a cumbersome task. Getting reservations is another and on top of that travelling with trunk and hold-all in an AC II tier or first class is another gambit. More over an army person has to carry at least four kinds of dresses/ uniforms and footwear.

Young officers should at all costs avoid the charms of smoking and drinking and smoking should be banned in Academies.

The Training Cycles

Next morning was a Sunday but in the Army it was a tradition to have 'Mandir Parade' on Sunday in the morning. That meant I had to get ready in the morning and be there in the mandir before other officers arrived at the mandir. Then the officers arrived one after another and I greeted them and then go and sit inside the mandir. Mandir in the army is essentially a sarva dharma sthal. The main deity may be Ganesh but on its sides you will have images of Jesus Christ, Mecca and Guru granth Saheb.

Officers JCOs and ORs all came to the mandir along with their families and it was customary for the bachelor officers to greet the ladies and have a kind conversation with them. All officers were standing outside the mandir and perhaps appreciating the excellent weather when somebody mentioned about the upcoming ITC (Individual Training Cycle) of A company.

Our second in Command told the Alpha company commander, " We will just sit in my office for 15 minutes and discuss it out." And guess what, I was posted as the company officer of A company. So there I was, attending the impromptu conference of the second in command with the A company commander and sitting there with my pen and dairy and taking down notes on issues that I failed to comprehend.

Just after two days I was sitting in a 3 Ton in the co drivers seat and moving to Hoshiyarpur where the ITC was to be conducted. Mobilising a company in a convoy was an important thing that I had learnt in the last 24 hours. There was an SOP (standard operating procedure) for mobilization which gave out load tables of the stores to be carried. There was a place earmarked for every item to be carried. There was three persons who were a must in every vehicle, viz, driver, co-driver and dandaman. The driver was supposed to focus on the road ahead, the co driver had to be alert to observe the area ahead like a lookout man and the dandaman was supposed to see the area behind and also the vehicle following. All vehicles were supposed to move in a convoy with interse distance between the vehicles kept to 5 to 10 metres depending on the road and the traffic. The dandaman carried a danda in his hand an he would signal to the driver by banging the danda on the body of the vehicle depending on the following vehicle when required to speed up or slow down.

I attended the ITC and the most interesting part for me was to conduct the firing. I was very strict with the range drills as these were necessary for the safety. I had memorized the range fire orders and conducted the firing according them. The painful part was to run with every firing detail to the butt and come back to the firing point. When I was in school in class 6, my father had got me an air rifle and I was good in firing that. In the academy I had not been able to fire well but here I was doing very well in firing. In the later time, about a year down I also got the best carbine firer at two occasions, once at the Brigade level and once at the Division level.

The ITC was for four weeks and on weekends the company commander would go back to the unit location as he was a married officer and the family was staying in the married accommodation at Kapurthala. I did not mind the company commander going back, but on weekends I was lonely at the camp location. Accomodation at the ITC location was in tents and I had a tent to myself but my personal belongings were few. In those days there were no mobile phones and the place where I was there was no STD phone nearby. I was not getting letters from anyone. But the ITC went off well.

After four weeks we came back from the ITC, but the next week the Bravo company ITC was starting. The Alpha company commander had given a good feedback on me and the company officer of Bravo company was on some course so I was requested, nay told to join the Bravo company ITC as well. I attended the Bravo company ITC in the same location as the Alpha company ITC. Great job, no accident and good training. We came back after a month. On coming back I asked for 20 days leave. I proceeded on leave and came back after 20 days. I reported back to the Adjutant and I was told that we were supposed to go on 'Op Alert' after 2 days and I should prepare my company for that. I barely got my uniforms ready and after two days we were off for the op alert.

Notes :

Having faith in god is a very important for every soldier. This gives the moral strength to sustain in long periods of isolation and in difficult conditions. It also prevents in helping him to control his passions and getting into wrong practices. Hence the tradition of having a Mandir Parade.

Young officers are traditionally groomed in the battalions to be able to converse respectfully with the ladies so that this trait of respecting the ladies remains with them lifelong.

The capability of moving a body of troops over long distances with requisite battle loads, by air, sea or land is one of the most important capability of a military leader.

Wars are fought at the Army level, battles are fought at the theatre level, but none can be won unless the troops are trained well at the company level.

The Night Patrol

I was a newly commissioned officer who had joined the unit just three months back. I had attended the individual training cycle at the Hoshiyarpur ranges and now I had come for Operational rehearsals to Attari. There were reportedly some terrorist moment in the area and we were to carry out domination of the area with day and night patrols. I was quite eager upon my soldiering and followed the patrolling program very religiously. It was just about my third patrol after reaching the area. We had started from the company op base at around 8 pm. The route from the patrols were being given from the brigade headquarters. I had marked the patrol on my map with a china graph pencil and I started according to that. There was a 20 feet wide canal flowing through our area of responsibility and after marching for about one hour we were supposed to cross the canal. The place where we were supposed to cross the nala there was no bridge to cross it. The nearest bridge was about 600 meters ahead. I was a young officer with no experience and I thought that the program was intentional to cross the canal at that point.

I insisted that we cross the nala at that point, and the troops obeyed. We all took our weapons towards our neck on our shoulder and one after another we got into the canal, and then crossed the canal. The entire patrol was on the other side of the canal. We were all drenched below our waist and the water had even soaked into our Double Molded Sole (DMS) boots. The month was November and the area was Punjab. Cold as it was we were lucky the water had not come above our waists. We quickened our pace. It was still about two hours before we reached our company op base. Our company senior JCO (Junior Commissioned officer) was waiting for us at the company gate. My radio operator had already informed him about the ordeal, I had made them go through.

Hot tea was ready at the post and we all filled our mugs and glasses. The Senior JCO stood in front of me with the motherly compassion of an Infantry senior JCO. The moment I finished my tea he told me to quickly go to my tent and change. He had ensured that a bukhari was lit inside my tent. In the meantime he shouted to my troops in tamil and they quickly scampered into their tents to change. The next morning I was supposed to run with the company cross country team. It was supposed to be 12 km for this day. I went and after finishing my cross country, I came back to my tent. The senior JCO was standing outside my tent. I could make out from his eyes that he wanted to talk to me about the previous night. I realized that it was a mistake to get into the water for no reason. Finally I spoke to him, " Kal raat ko ham sab bheeg gaye." To which he said, "Ha saab, Naya jaga par paani mein nahi utarna chahiye."

At lunch time when I went to the officers mess, all my seniors were waiting for me and the beer was on me for taking the troops into water.

Notes :

The best thing about the troops is that they will obey your orders because you are their commander. It is important for you to stand true on their faith and lead them honestly.

Subedar Major and Senior JCO are two very important appointments to form a link between the Officers and the Jawans to see the Adm requirements and the tasking.

Conference at Brigade Headquarters

I had been about two months at the op alert when there was an op conference at the Brigade Headquarters, all officers were to attend and I was also attending.

In those days the insurgency in Punjab was still active and they discussed various operations for controlling the situation. Towards the end of the discussion the Brigade commander said, " Let's have the inputs from the young officers and they caught me sitting in the last row. I was called to the front and asked to give my inputs.

I said that the patrolling program which was issued from the brigade headquarters was not effective. Suddenly I had everyone looking at me but the Brigade commander intervened and asked me to continue.

I said that the program was every night covering a distance of 10 to 12 kilometers on map. Since this was being done on foot it had some disadvantages. Firstly our approach to the villages was marred by the dogs barking in the village, and so all surprise was lost, also it was not practicable to be marching 10 to 12 kilometers every night.

Secondly if while approaching the village we saw a vehicle moving out of the village, there was nothing that we could do. So it was more practical if we had some vehicle mounted patrols, so that we could reach the village with surprise and also give a chase if required. I was not sure I had done the right thing but it was much appreciated by the brigade commander. The op alert continued.

Notes :

Young officers should put across their points in a subtle manner without sounding snobbish.

It was very good on the part of the Brigade Commander to take inputs and appreciate them.

The Jonga Rammed

I was about four weeks into the Attari Op Alert. We had almost settled down. The troops had cleaned the bunkers on the Ditch cum bund, and we were moving on to practicing various battle drills. One Saturday I got the message that some guests were coming from the division headquarters on the next day, which was a Sunday. I was supposed to meet them in civvies and take them around on the Ditch Cum Bund (DCB) and take them to the company view point and arrange some refreshments for them. I went to the designated point. I was in my Jonga along with my driver and two jawans armed with their Self Loading Rifles. After a while a car came along and stopped at our check post. I glanced at the number of the car given to me and just then three young ladies came out of the car and asked for me. They were all in their twenties, around my age and were all wearing T shirts and trousers. I was like swept off my feet as I shook my hands with them I introduced myself and ushered them to sit at the view point that had been done up. We offered them refreshments as they asked me how life was over there on the DCB.

As we talked they looked at my open Jonga and requested for a ride in the open Jonga. For once I felt sorry for myself. I had never driven a four wheeler before. I said yes, but they would have to sit in the rear seat where the gun was mounted for operations and they were thrilled. I sat in the co-drivers seat and the three beauties sat on the rear seats while my driver drove us along the DCB. And after about half an hour came back to the view point from where we had started. They got down and we said good byes. They got into the car and drove off.

I was just 18 months of military training at the Indian Military Academy, less than six months of commissioned service and this encounter with three young ladies had played havoc with my hormones.

I decided that I had to learn how to drive and I had to do it now. I told the driver that I will drive the Jonga and that he should sit in the co driver seat. He retorted that the Commanding Officer will punish him if he allowed me to drive, but I was all adrenalin and got into the driver seat. The poor chap got into the co driver seat and the two escorts got into the rear seats.

The Jonga was a beast of the vehicle. I put the ignition key and twisted. The engine coughed and the vehicle jumped and stopped. The driver told me that I should release the clutch and brake slowly and at the same time press the accelerator as I engage the first gear. I did the same and the Jonga started moving, slowly at first and thereafter with speed. I pressed the clutch and engaged the second gear and the Jonga took speed. The track on the DCB had the bund on one side and a steep drop on the other. Besides there were huge trees all along the dussi and the track curved from right to left and left to right along the DCB.

I had just driven about 150 meters and engaged the third gear and just then the track curved on to the right and I rammed the Jonga into the tree ahead. I was on the steering wheel so I held on to the steering wheel tight and had the minimum shock. The two persons sitting behind jumped off their seats and sustained minor injuries. But my poor driver hit his chin on the dashboard and got a cut on his chin. The Jonga had stopped and I too got off the Jonga, but the driver had slumped like the captain of a sinking ship, bleeding from his chin. I walked back to the check post with shaking knees , got on to the 5 B telephone and informed our second in command about the accident as our commanding officer was on leave at that time. Along came an ambulance and the recovery and we were taken to the field hospital Where the driver received 7 stitches while the three of us got away with medicines.

I was to go on leave for Diwali the next week, but my leave was cancelled and it was to be decided after the CO returned back from leave. They were trying to avoid the court of inquiry, so I paid for the repairs of the Jonga from the civil workshop, which in those days cost me about two months salary.

The commanding officer came back from leave and the first thing he did was to send me on leave. Thereafter I got some time to prepare for my young officers course and went for the young officers course.

Notes:

It is important to trust the young officers and train them in driving. In current day scenario they may be coaxed to attend private driving classes in the civil driving schools.

The Football Matches

I had completed my young officers course and joined back the unit. I found that the inter battalion football matches were on. I was not a keen footballer but since I was there I had to play and it so happened that we won the matches. Now the brigade football team was selected and the same was to go to Amritsar to play the division level matches.

So the next week, there I was in Amritsar with the brigade football team to play the football matches. I was not Ronaldo, but I was the team captain and I had to justify my detailment.

There was a Junior Commissioned Officer (JCO) from my unit who was very good in playing football so I gave him the authority to coach the team, but I made sure I played all the matches including the practice matches, and also went to see the matches of our rival teams. One good tip I gave my team was if you are playing against the gorkha team, don't let the ball get into the air and if you are playing against the mallus, don't allow the ball to roll on the ground. Our team reached the semifinals and we won the semifinals. Now this was great news. This meant we were going to play the finals.

The Brigade Headquarters sent one officer with some JCOs and jawans to cheer us up in the finals. The officer who came did his best to do some last minute, on the spot coaching of my football team. The opposing team had some gorkha troops and was tough. We reached the tie breaker at 1:1 and some extraw time. My JCO got injured and we lost the finals.

Notes:

Giving initiative to the competent works.

Trying to overshadow the competent can be counterproductive.

FUP Marking

This was my second Op Alert in the area of Punjab. This time it was a bigger one. We were rehearsing the attack across the DCB. I was the IO and I was to be doing the FUP marking of our unit. But then they decided that FUP marking was to be done at the Brigade level and since I had been sincere in my football at the Brigade level they tasked me to do the FUP marking for the entire brigade. It was planned that the Brigade would attack two battalions up and after attacking across the DCB they would provide a safe corridor for the Mechanised Infantry crossing followed by the Tank crossing.

Then some one mentioned that the FUP marking should be done by using LED instead of muffled torches, so that it will assist in the later crossings as well. I was tasked to give a demonstration and funds were allotted for the same.

FUP marking and the Brigade Assault were a later part, but the first thing was the rehearsals. As a first step I was supposed to lay out the Brigade FUP marking stores and then these were to be inspected by the Brigade Commander. I asked the Brigade Major as to what time the Brigade Commander would come to inspect the stores and he gave me a time of 0900 hrs. Accordingly I gave a time of 0830 hrs to the troops who were a part of the FUP marking party. I had half an hour to make some corrections before the Brigade Commander came.

It was 1000 hrs and the Brigade commander had not yet come. I asked the adjutant as to when the Brigade Commander would come. He said " Oh what's the hurry man. He must be busy." I called again at 1230 hrs only to get another rebuke. The question was not of me alone, there were three FUP marking parties of the three units waiting there with me and they had to be sent to their unit cookhouses for their lunch. After some time I took an independent decision and sent the troops in two batches for their lunch. They also fetched the lunch for me.

That evening there was supposed to be a party at the canal, where all officers would be present and the Brigade Commander was also invited. It was 1730 hrs now and the Brigade commander had not yet come to inspect the FUP marking stores. As a lieutenant I would speak only to the Adjutant and now even he was not available on the phone. I was not sure that the Brigade Commander was coming and I could not wind up on my own. But I did not want to miss the party either. I kept two Jawans from each unit and one JCO along with the FUP marking stores and sent everyone else back. At 2000 hrs I myself left the place and went to the place where the party was being held.

All officers were in civil dress and I had come in combat dress. After some hesitation I picked up a glass of beer and started locating myself in the party. I soon came to know that the Brigade Commander had also not been able to come till then.

I was about to finish my first mug when suddenly the Brigade commander came in from somewhere and he came straight to me and put a hand on my shoulder and asked, " So Parag, how are you." My response was "Sorry Sir, You are late."

Suddenly there was a pin drop silence and the three commnding officers who were approaching the Brigade commander disappeared from there. The Brigade Commander was very kind and said, "O yaar, kya ho gaya". I then went on to explain how I had been standing with my troops, the whole day and there was no response from the staff.

He explained that he had been with the GOC all day long and hence could not come in time, but he promised to see the stores after the party. And then he himself took one mug of beer and told the waiter to refill my mug as well. Cheers was with me.

The FUP marking stores were inspected by the Brigade commander at midnight and it was 1 am by the time I returned to my tent.

Notes:

Resounding support of the senior officers is a very good morale booster.

Claymore Mine

This was one of the episodes in the early years of my service. I had less than three years of service at that time. I was with my unit in J & K and we were deployed on the line of control in the Kilo Bravo sector. Charlie company was deployed at Seira Bravo which was bang on the line of control. The company commander of Seira Bravo post had to go on leave so I was told to go and take over the company. The complete company was deployed on a single post which was just two to three hundred meters from the enemy post as the crow flies. It had well entrenched defenses with overhead protection. The enemy post was situated at a greater height than our own post. So you could say that they were overlooking our defenses.

I walked down to the post with my troops and settled down in the company commander's bunker which was in the center of the post.

Stand to was being religiously followed at first light and last light and I inspected the defenses during stand to. There was no electricity or generator at the post so we were on kerosene or wick lamps. I finished my dinner at 8.30 and settled into my sleeping bag as there was nothing much to do. There were two dogs at the post. At about 9.30 pm the dogs started barking. I was always curious whenever the dogs barked at night. I believed that they always barked because they could either see farther that I could see or they could smell or hear better than I could. Either ways there had to be something. Some reason why they were barking. I again put on my combat dress and shoes and called the duty NCO to take me around the defenses. I went around the defenses and almost the same time the dogs stopped barking.

After my walk around the defenses I asked him as to why the dogs had been barking. He said that they bark intermittently during the night and especially so after dinner time. Next night again the same pattern followed. The dogs barked and I went around the defenses. The third night I decided to observe so I put a chair on my bunker at 9 pm and sat on it. It was pitch dark so it was difficult to see anything. In those days there were no night vision devices, neither with us nor the enemy. Again at about 9.30 pm the dogs started barking. They barked for about 10 minutes and then stopped barking. This much time was enough for me to see the direction in which they were barking. Next morning I called the CHM and went out in the defenses in the direction in which the dogs were barking.

The area was exactly ahead of the MMG bunker. There were no wire obstacles ahead but I was told that the area was littered with mines, laid around 20 years back. The area ahead of the MMG bunker was a 600 meter slope with pine trees and, thick undergrowth, leading down to the nala to the left side of the post. Since this was the forward most post on the line of control there were no patrols going ahead of this post. Again at night the dogs barked and I could not sit tight on the dogs barking. Next morning I set out on an adventurous plan. We had some claymore mines in the ammunition bunker and I decided to use one of them. I got two insulated copper wires and one empty thread roll. Took one disposable battery of the a radio set. Taking all this material in a rug sack I set out on a patrol. I climbed up the ridge on the own side and then went off the track into the jungle. We went cross country till we reached a nala in the re-entrant, running down from the top. Thereafter we went down the nala for about 400 meters. This was about the area towards where the dogs barked every night. Although I was not sure it was a trail, but I found the area was open for someone to move. I selected four big trees to set up my trap.

Handling a claymore mine itself was a dangerous work. It fires a lethal hail of steel pellets over an angle of fifty to sixty degrees. The mine had to be set up next to a tree with the fuse fitted. Then the battery had to be connected with the claymore mine and the adhoc switch in series. The last thing was to connect the trip wire to the adhoc switch and taken around two trees ahead of the claymore mine and fixed to the fourth tree. After that we had to cross the killing area and come out behind the claymore mine. It took us about 40 minutes to set up the whole thing and come out of the area. I climbed back along the nala and came back to my post.

Routine at the post continued and the two dogs continued to bark intermittently at night and nothing happened.

After a few days the original company commander came back and I briefed him about the operation claymore mine. There after I was side stepped to the neighboring company. It was barely 4 days I had gone to the neighboring company that on night at around 9.30 pm there was a huge blast in the forest. There was immediate stand-to at all posts. It was probably in the area where I had put the claymore mine.

Next morning the company commander took out the same troops that had gone with me to put up the claymore mine. They reached the area and found that the mine had blasted. They could not find anything else, but one thing was for sure, the ad-hoc switch had worked and the claymore mine had blasted.

Notes:

In counter infiltration ops the results may not be immediately acclaimable, but deterrence on the enemy has to be a continuous effort.

Fire Assault on Papa Charlie

It was summer season and we were deployed on the line of control. Every second day, there were reports of terrorists having infiltrated through our area, and gone into the rear areas. It was very frustrating in every conference at the battalion headquarters. In every Intelligence report there was one place that figured very regularly, and that was Papa Charlie. Papa Charlie comprised of two dhoks which were located close to the nala on the other side of line of control. On the own side was the Kilo spur which ran down from the Kilo Bravo top. There was an abandoned village comprising of five to six huts at kilo bravo one which was about 40 minutes down from Kilo Bravo top. It was said that it was vacated as there was incessant firing from the enemy side a year or so back.

 I was posted at Kilo Bravo and I took it upon myself to sort out the problem of Papa Charlie which was being used as a launch pad. I took a patrol from Kilo Bravo to Kilo One village. From Kilo One village there was a small track moving ahead on the Kilo One spur. I was told that this track went to Kilo One forward where there used to be a section post earlier which had to be vacated due to incessant enemy shelling. I went with my patrol up to the abandoned picket at Kilo One forward.

There were two dilapidated bunkers with heavy undergrowth in the area. Our records showed that there was a minefield in the area ahead. There was so much shrub and undergrowth over there that the idea of reviving Kilo One forward to dominate Papa Charlie was not tenable. Moreover Papa Charlie was not directly visible from there.

I returned back to the abandoned Kilo One village and started observing Papa Charlie. The two dhoks at Papa Charlie were empty but the area surrounding them was clear of any undergrowth. This was an indication that some one was using the place. This place was not under observation from Kilo Bravo or from kilo One forward, but it was under observation from the abandoned Kilo One village. I decided that it was necessary to occupy the abandoned Kilo One village with a platoon post over there. I discussed the same with the second in command of our battalion. He advised me to further recce the area before we came up with a plan.

 The following few days I went to Kilo One every day and kept the area under observation.

The area to the left of the track between Kilo One and Kilo One forward was a steep slope with tall trees and interspersed with thick undergrowth. Moving a little ahead on this slope I realized that this was one hell of an approach from Kilo One to Papa Charlie or vice versa. Very difficult but possible. We had thick nylon ropes in the company which were used to picket the tracks in heavy snow during winters. I could use these ropes to climb down from Kilo One to Papa Charlie. I decided that it was essential to occupy Kilo One and before doing that it was essential to destroy the Dhoks at Papa Charlie with rocket launchers.

I asked for volunteers for this high risk mission from among my troops and selected four of them. Armed with our personal weapon, we carried one rocket launcher and four rounds of High Explosive ammunition, and the nylon rope to climb down. We waited at the top of the spur till 2 pm. When the sun went on the reverse slope we let down the rope and climbed down the steep slope. It was about 85 degrees and it took us about 40 minutes to reach the bottom. In fact the rope was a little short and we had to climb down the last 10 meters holding on to the undergrowth There were three large trees where we could take cover and fire the rockets on the dhoks. We took up position and waited. The time for the assault was decided to be at 1630 hours so that we had we had enough time and light to climb up the slope and get back to safety.

There was no movement towards Papa Charlie and the dhoks seemed to be empty. None the less the rockets had to be fired and the dhoks destroyed. The rocket launcher has a big backblast and there was very little space for me to stand. I stood behind one of the three large trees . This was about four meters behind the tree from where the rocket launcher was to be fired, so the back blast was going to come in my direction. But that was just excitement as I was sure this tree was big enough to give me protection.

At exactly 4.30 pm we fired the first rocket which skimmed the roof of the dhok and burst into the hillside behind the dhok. I could feel the warmth of the backblast going on to my right. The jawan with the rocket launcher compressed himself against the tree a little more, gave some correction on the launcher and fired the other three rockets with which the dhoks were completely destroyed and even caught fire. Immidiately it was time to pack up things and move back. It took us just ten minutes to climb up the rope which had taken us 40 minutes to climb down.

The next morning we started the reconstruction of the Kilo One post and we constructed 6 bunkers in the next one month. Papa Charlie stopped figuring in the intelligence reports.

Safe Lane on November Spur

I was again posted at Kilo Bravo and now that the post at Kilo One was established, my eyes rolled down on to November Spur. November spur was a two kilometer long spur that rolled down from Kilo Bravo in the Northern direction. There were tall pine trees interspersed with undergrowth on the spur. At some places there were rocky patches and the western slopes were interspersed with some bald patches. At the point where the November spur dipped into the nala, It overlooked the loading point post in the area occupied by the neighboring country. However the loading point and the post were not visible from Kilo Bravo post. I wanted to go to November spur and see both these . But there were minefields on the November spur. Old minefields laid after 1971. These mines had probably shifted due to snow falling and melting on them every year. Because of these mines there were no patrols going on the November spur. But the area up to the lowest point on the November spur was in our area of responsibility, and I wanted to see it and walk it with my own feet.

Besides whatever came to Papa Charlie was coming from this loading point. I discussed the same with our second in command. He said the idea was good but how will you go to November spur. To that my answer was ready. I said I will make a safe lane on November spur. Making a safe lane on November spur was no joke. It was mid October now. We decided to make a safe lane by end October and launch a fire assault on the loading point by first week of November.

Walking into the minefield was a risky job so I wanted good volunteers for that. I selected about eight men for that and started the work. We had to go very deliberately as I did not want to take any casualty due to mine blast. More over making a safe lane for two kilometers was not a joke. I ensured that I was personally present on ground with the front troops who were doing the prodding to remove the mines. We removed about 8 anti personal mines over a period of eight days and by 31 Oct the lane was ready to be used by us. We decided to launch the assault on 04th of November. This time we needed permission from higher headquarters as the assault would attract international attention. On 3rd November I carried out the final recce. I had finally seen the loading point and the mule track. There were two wooden buildings over there. The permission from higher headquarters was still awaited.

On 4 th of November I moved along with eight soldiers along the safe lane on the November spur. After about 1500 meters I told 4 of them to take up position over there. I took the balance four carrying 84 mm Rocket launcher and 4 rounds of HE ammunition with me to the vantage point.

 The permission from the higher headquarters had not yet arrived, and our second in command had instructed me to check back before firing. The intended time of assault was 1430 hrs and the time now was 1200 hrs. When we started in the morning, there was bright sunlight. But now the valley on the opposite side was filled with dark clouds. At about 1400 hrs our second in command came on the radio set and categorically informed me that the permission had been denied, and that I should fall back. It dampened my spirit but then we had to move back. I told my troops to pack up and we started moving back. Just then the wind started blowing and the dark clouds started moving in our direction. Just as we started moving towards Kilo Bravo, it started snowing on November spur and our tracks were covered with snow. I went on leave on 07 Nov and when I came back I was posted to a different location.

Speculative Firing

Kilo Romeo was a village that came before you climbed upto Zulu saddle coming up from the division headquarters side. There was a rear location at Kilo Romeo along with a detachment of the vehicle repair workshop. This rear location was well protected. But ahead of the Kilo Romeo garrison, there was a bridge. This bridge was a key location and had to be defended from any terrorist action. So there was one platoon deployed over there for the protection of the bridge while the rest of the company was deployed around the main Kilo Romeo garrison where the rear locations of the army were located, for its protection.

This bridge at Kilo Romeo was so important that there were orders for one officer to stay at the platoon on Kilo Romeo bridge. I as a Captain was chosen for this, while one Major stayed at the main garrison of Kilo Romeo.

The space at the bridge was quite limited. My room was next to the road, so much so that one could come on a bicycle and lob a grenade into the bed. There were two rooms for the jawans behind my room and one room in the house across the road on the first floor. Beyond this house was a depression with some open fields.

On going to the bridge post the first thing that I had to do was to enhance the security of my living space. 'Jaan hai to jahan hai'. There were some empty barrels lying in the rear so I got them stacked in front of my window. Nights were generally quiet but at around 10 pm in the night there were dogs barking across the fields in the broken ground beyond the road. Although our sentries were alert I was not happy with the dogs barking in the far distance. After about a week I decided to sort out the matter. The bridge post had one line telephone coming from the main garrison in the rear location. We could communicate both ways through this telephone only. Besides this there was one long distance Radio set and two small range radio sets to be used for patrols and in case of an emergency.

So the next day I gave orders to disconnect the telephone at 9.50 pm and also switch off the Radio set at the same time. I brought the post to stand-to and myself got on to the top of the house across the road where we had one room. I had already chosen a place to put the LMG. So I mounted the LMG and fired two magazines from it in the direction where the dogs were barking. After some time I connected the telephone and called up the company commander at the rear location that the telephone had temporarily malfunctioned and there were dogs barking so we had to resort to speculative firing.

Notes:

Firing of the weapon was done just to create a deterrent for the militants.

Chasing a Lone Militant

I was posted in the Mike sector and I was the company commander at India Bravo. Since I was to study for my staff college entrance exam I was left at India Bravo so that I could devote my time to studying.

Captain Seira Bravo was the adjutant and he was at Delta location at the Tactical HQ. Delta, Charlie Zulu and India Bravo were all located in the valley along the nala. On the other side of Delta the nala moved towards Tango Seira. Before Tango Seira was the area of Black Rock about half an hour climb from Delta loc. Since Capt Seira Bravo was to go on leave and he was to hand over to another officer. He took a patrol with the other officer towards the Black Rock. It was just about 8 am and the day was bright.

As they were climbing towards black rock they could see a lone person sitting on the knoll at Black Rock. From far he looked like a shepherd, but there were no sheep to be seen around. As they kept climbing and came closer, they were also cautious. When they were about 100 meters from this person Capt Seira Bravo halted the patrol and called him and told him to put his hands up. To their surprise this man got up and fired two bursts of AK 47 towards the patrol, and ran into the jungle. Our troops immediately took cover and returned fire. The matter was reported to the commanding officer and more troops were mobilized from Delta location, and Charlie Zulu. Tango sera company commander was told to put stops. The Commanding Officer also started for Black Rock with his QRT. Since India Bravo was further off I was not called. So I got on to the radio set and requested the Commanding Officer if I could also join the search operation. The permission was granted and I took a patrol of 7 persons and started at about noon from India Bravo. At around 4.30 pm I reached the area of Black Rock. A small bivouac had been put at that place and the Commanding Officer was sitting inside it on the ground sheet. As I reached the place, the Commanding Officer called me to come and sit down beside him while he called his orderly and told him to get some tea for me. While the orderly went to get tea, I told the Commanding Officer that I will just look around and come. I told my troops that we will move up another 50 meters and come back. As we started up the scout in my patrol fired one burst and halted. Immediately everyone went to the ground, but there was no return fire. I moved ahead to the scout and asked him what had happened. He had seen a man in blue kafni, about 100 meters up and fired one burst towards him. As per him this person jumped into the undergrowth and ran down the valley towards Tango Sierra and ran away. So we took position on the rocky ledge that climbed up from Black Rock. The valley towards Tango Seirra could be seen from there but soon it was last light and we took up positions to establish stops on the ridge line. Further search could be carried out only after first light, ie. next morning. We had kept the area ahead under observation. At around mid night, it appeared to us as though we saw a small glow, something akin to a muffled torch in the forest below. A rocket launcher would have been the ideal weapon to fire in this situation but we were not carrying one. We made do with lobbying some grenades and firing LMG into the forest. Rest of the night was quiet and in the morning I started my search into the forest. The climb down was quite steep. We reached the area where we had fired. We could not find any trail. The valley on the other side opened towards Mike Bravo, which was supposed to be a bahek which was used by the bakarwals when they came grazing their sheep in the summers. I decided to search the area right down up to the nala. This was a steep nala running down and there was still about 2 feet of snow in the nala. The area on the sides was very steep and there was loose gravel which was slippery as well. I decided that we will slide down the nala on the snow and then traverse on to the side, from where we could walk further. I took my AK 47 in dhava position close to my chest and sat down on the snow and started sliding down the snow. I had to slide down around 50 to 60 meters, before I encountered a fallen tree trunk on which I could thrust my feet and stand up. My troops followed the same and we finally reached the bottom of the valley. The main nala came from Mike Bravo's bahek over here. I kept my patrol in the tree line and observed the area for about 30 minutes before moving ahead into the open. I reached on the other side of the nala and to my surprise I found a sangarh like structure, made by piling up stones on top of one another. There was no overhead protection but it was made under a huge tree and provided for good all round protection. I wondered who had made this and who was using this. There were no tell tale marks over there and I decided to use it for the day. Brigadier Romeo was the brigade commander and he decided to join the operation. He was to come in vehicles by road up to Tango Seirra and then walk along the nala and walk up to my location as I was the farthest on this side. We were on radio contact and I decided to meet him at the sangarh. I told my troops to camouflage themselves among the trees and I myself sat in the sangarh, waiting for his patrol to come over. There was no way anyone, who would come from that side, could have seen us till even they crossed our area. It was a perfect ambush site. I was on radio contact with the commander's patrol and when the Brigadier was just about 50 meters from the sangarh. I told them to halt and that I would be approaching them now. I along with my radio buddy got up and went ahead to greet and receive him.

When I brought him to the sangarh he was mighty thrilled. And then he decided he will stay there for the night. A link patrol was organised from Tango Seira to get hot meals for the commander which included chicken and roti and of course a bottle of old monk. The next morning the commander told us to terminate the operation. I decided to move with him upto Tango Seirra. On my advice we took the route through the forest.

The scouts in his personal bodyguards had AK 47 rifles with under barrel grenade launcher. We had been walking for about 20 minutes when one of his scouts had an accidental handling of the weapon due to which one grenade from the under barrel grenade launcher slipped off the weapon and fell a few meters ahead. I was not sure weather it got primed or not but we all froze and went to the ground. And guess what the Brigadier was the first to move. He got ahead, picked up the grenade and hurled it into the nala. It did not explode so I guess it had not got primed, but then we destroyed it in situ using some plastic explosive. Just then we got a message on the radio that a man in blue kafni had been apprehended in the nala close to Tango Seirra. He was not in possession of a weapon and he would not speak so we handed him over to the police and the operation was terminated.

The Convoy along Barrack River

I once had the opportunity of shifting the entire formation headquarters from South Assam to Manipur by road. I was posted as a staff officer in the headquarters and the headquarters was to be moved by road through the Barrack valley. The road along the Barrack river was one which was in most disuse. The road ran along the Barrack river and there were umpteen number of bridges. Many of these bridges were very narrow and some even had iron plates which would move out of position when any vehicle crossed the bridge. The next vehicle had to realign the plate before crossing the bridge. There was one BSF post at the last bridge which was a little larger and was called as the Barrack Bridge. There was just one CRPF post short of the Barrack Bridge. For the rest of the journey we were on our own up to Jiribam.

The load tables showed a load of 50 vehicles. That was a huge convoy. In the time when the headquarters was to be shifted, most of the officers were on temp duty or leave so it finally came down to taking the convoy with only three officers. One was self, the second was a Major and the third was a Colonel on the last leg of his service. It was decided that I will lead the convoy while the Major will get the rear of the convoy. There were only two vehicles moving with the convoy. The first was a Gypsy, which was given to me and the second was a jonga which was given to the Major. The colonel preferred to sit in a shaktiman, a famous army truck with 3 ton load carrying capacity and tremendous mobility in mountain terrain.

It was decided to start the convoy at midnight, ie 0001 am, cross Jiribam before first light and then reach Imphal by 1600 hrs. But 50 vehicles was a big convoy . I was to lead and navigation was on service maps. At the time when we were to start there was total chaos. The convoy could be lined up only at 1.00 am and the Major reached at that time only. His jonga was fully loaded including his radio operator and driver. When he came he was a bit upset and wanted to start immediately. I had radio communication with everyone in the convoy, but the communication with the major was not through. Since it was a long convoy I wanted to keep the convoy together I reduced the speed of the leading vehicle to 30 km/hour. In the meantime I was taking report from all the radio operators in the convoy who were seated in every tenth vehicle. The others responded but the fifth on who was in the Majors vehicle would not respond. I ran the convoy for about 30 minutes and then halted the convoy to regain control. I was not sure the last ten vehicles had fetched up as they were not in contact. After 15 minutes the Major drove up to my Gypsy and he was furious as to why I had stopped the convoy. I explained to him that his radio operator was not in communication and so I had halted the convoy but he would not listen.

I resumed the convoy and increased the speed to 40 km/ hour. After about 5 am we had come into the area where we had started crossing the bridges on Barrack river. There was little road space and the speed was restricted so I moved the convoy slow and steady. I had been getting reports from four radio operators, but the Majors radio operator was still out of communication. Finally at 12 noon I crossed the main Barrack Bridge. Ahead was a three kilometer long road which climbed up gently towards Nonei, and there was enough space to halt the convoy and have lunch break. It was almost 3 pm by the time most of the convoy had fetched up. I could see all the vehicles lined up from where I stood. I was told by the fourth radio operator that the last four vehicles had not fetched up. I went back in my gypsy to take stock. In between I met the colonel whom I had to search. He wanted to keep the convoy moving. I told him to not to move the convoy till such time I came back. I went down the convoy. The last vehicle was about 500 meters from the Barrack Bridge, but the report was the same. There were four vehicles which had not fetched up. One shaktiman truck with broken axle, one recovery, one shaktiman truck with the protection party and the major's vehicle. I went further down upto the Barrack Bridge. There was a CRPF Post at the bridge. I met the JCO in charge of the post and told him that these four vehicles will be coming and he should tell them to stay there for the night. At least they should leave the off road vehicle with the broken axle over there and join the convoy.

I was just talking to the JCO when I happened to look towards the road and to my horror, the entire convoy had vanished. I asked them on the radio set and they told me that the Colonel had ordered the convoy to keep moving slowly.

So here I was standing on the Barrack bridge with the entire convoy having moved ahead and four vehicles , yet to fetch up, which were totally out of communication.

In my gypsy there were two huge boxes loaded, containing the documents of operational importance, so there was no place for any protection or troops to sit. So it was only me and my driver. My job was to lead the convoy, so I had to move ahead. I sat in the gypsy and told the driver to move on. So here I was standing at the barrack bridge. Just my driver and me in one gypsy, carrying two huge boxes of documents. The convoy had moved on under the orders of the colonel, and the Major had not yet fetched up. One lonely road with dense jungle on both sides. I got into the gypsy and told the driver to chase the convoy.

The next village to be encountered was perhaps Nonei, but the convoy under the self stewardship of the front vehicle had already crossed Nonei. At the starting of the village was a bamboo barrier which was open so we drove in to the village. Inside the road went through the market. My driver who was a local from Manipur said that good quality chilly was available in the market and he wanted to buy some . I could see the exit barrier in front. I told him to halt the vehicle and go and buy the stuff he wanted. There was a hotel by the side of the road. I got out of the vehicle and purchased the   one bottle of water and came back to the gypsy. My driver came and we moved on. There was no communication with the Major and the convoy had moved ahead. The next check point would be Khopum, where there was an Assam Rifles company. The post at Khopum was on a hill. Fortunately the convoy had halted at the company, and I was told the colonel was sitting at the company view point along with the Assam Rifles company commander. I too went up to the view point and joined them. We had some biscuits and tea while the company commander gave pack meals for the troops. Regaining command and control of a 50 vehicle convoy was a herculean task. The area ahead was again a forbidden territory. Jungle terrain with terrorist camps. It was already getting dark again. I decided to drag the convoy ahead. The Assam Rifles company commander assured me that he would keep the off road vehicle there at his post and urge the Major to join the convoy ahead. I got into the Gypsy and moved on.

In the meantime the Major along with the rear echelon had moved ahead with the rear echelon. He crossed the Barrack Bridge and moved towards Nonei. All four vehicles drove   into the village and moved through the market. The bamboo barrier at the exit of the market was closed. The Major halted the Jonga and got out of the vehicle to open the barrier.

At this time some terrorists of one of the militant outfits had come to the market and they were doing tax collection on behalf of the terrorist outfit. They were surprised when the Major came out of the Gypsy with weapon in hand, to open the barrier and started looking towards the shops in the market. But they didn't stop at that. They opened fire on the Major. The protection vehicle was the last. So in between the protection vehicle and the Majors vehicle there was the recovery along with the shaktiman truck with the broken axle. They could not see the terrorists from where they were but they on hearing the firing dismounted and deployed on the ground. The Majors driver got a bullet in the first burst and he went and ducked behind the tyre of the recovery truck. The Major got towards the other side and got into the drivers seat and started the Jonga. In the bargain he got two gunshot wounds, one in the stomach and one in the foot. As the jonga started moving it attracted more gunfire from the terrorists. The Major managed to drive the vehicle for about four kilometers and pulled over to the side and halted. He soon fell unconscious. In the meantime the radio operator with the recovery vehicle got onto the frequency of the signal regiment and informed the headquarters staff, about the ambush. After a short while the company commander from Khopum reached the site where the Majors Jonga was parked by the road. The Major was bleeding and in a swoon. The Radio operator and the Major's buddy had passed out.

After the initial fire the terrorists had left and the protection party marched ahead of the three vehicles and moved out from Nonei. The Major's driver was put into the Shaktiman truck. In the meantime I was ordered to move back and evacuate the Major on priority. I turned my Gypsy and moved in the direction of Khopum. A second encounter on the same road on the same night was unlikely and within half an hour I reached Khopum. At the same time the casualties reached Khopum.

The Major had two gun shot wounds, one in the leg and one in the stomach. The major's driver had received a gunshot wound in the shoulder and he stayed at Khopum. The radio operator and the Major's buddy had succumbed to their injuries. The Major was put into the Assam Rifles ambulance and that tagged along with my vehicle. He was evacuated by road throughout the night and reached the military hospital the next morning. The driver was evacuated by helicopter the next morning.

I reached the military hospital along with the Major at 6 AM in the morning. The team of doctors was ready at the hospital and I knew the Major was in good hands. The convoy followed under the Colonel and closed in by afternoon. The Major had to be hospitalized for about a month and he recovered totally.

Gypsy Toppled

Now this was about 10 years after I had rammed my Jonga into a tree. This time I had been sent to a place called Tango for internal security duties. The month was January and there was a mela(fair) which was to be held after one week. People from various parts of the country were to come for the mela and I was there with my company to provide security for the mela. The site of the mela was reconnoitered by me and we had decided on the strategy for providing security for the mela.

It was on the first day that I had reached there and in the evening I was told that in addition to the security there was a medical camp which was to be organized at the mela. A medical officer was to come there from the brigade headquarters and I was supposed to take the medical officer with me to the site of the mela and carry out a joint recce for the siting of the medical camp.

 The medical officer arrived at Tango at about 11 am. She had come in a one ton ambulance which would move slowly in the hills. By this time I had been driving the army vehicles off and on so I decided to drive her in my Gypsy to the mela site and carry out the joint recce. It was essential to carry the two nursing assistants who had come along with her to the site and I had to carry two armed escorts, plus the driver. I decided to drive with the medical officer in the co-driver seat and the rest of the paraphernalia ie 5 persons in the vertical rear seats of the gypsy. The road to the site of the mela was a gradual climb and the gypsy rode smoothly in the first and the second gear to the site of the mela. We carried out the recce and started back towards Tango. The gypsy was overloaded and this time it was moving downhill. I drove for some time in the first gear and put the second gear. After just 5 minutes I reached a place where the road had a sharp hairpin bend to the left. I pressed on to the brake pedal and at the same time turned the steering wheel to the left. At that instance I realized that the left two wheels of the gypsy lifted off the ground and the Gypsy started toppling. There were 5 persons in the backseat and there was nothing I could do to stop the Gypsy from toppling. I knew very well that the gypsy was going to topple on the driver side and I was in the driver seat. I held on to the steering wheel tightly with my right hand and saved the doctor from falling on to me or the steering wheel with my left hand and the Gypsy fell on its side.

Eventually we all got off the Gypsy. I was the last to get out after switching off the ignition key. None of us were injured. We pushed the gypsy back on its wheels , sat in the gypsy and drove back to Tango. The gypsy had got very bad scratch marks on the right side. In fact the entire surface was scratched. We had lunch with the medical team and the medical officer left after giving us a strip of paracetamol, just in case we had body ache. Off course in case of a headache we were supposed to report at the field hospital. After the doctor left my senior JCO looked at me, but I smiled and said " Not to worry, not to worry, we will get it right."

I picked up the phone and spoke to my commanding officer and told him about the visit by the doctor and recce of the mela site and siting of the medical camp. He said "Good". Then I told him , on the way back there was a small mishap. The gypsy toppled on its side and got scratched on the right side, but no one got injured. He asked me, who was driving, I said me. He was suddenly silent on his side and I could hear his breathing on the phone. He asked me about the doctor and I said that she had left after having lunch with us. Next he asked how big was the scratch and I told him that the complete right side was scratched. After that I heard the choosiest of adjectives from him. Finally he gave me 48 hours to get the gypsy in shape and that too at my own cost and slammed the phone. I got the gypsy repaired and repainted, though it took me 3 – 4 days but don't ask me how many months salary went there. Only God's blessing was that no one had got injured and there was no court of inquiry.

Search of Kilo Forest

The mela ahead of Tango went on smoothly. I was hoping to move back to the battalion after the mela along with my company, but so far there were no orders for de-induction. On the 17th of January, I called up my commanding officer to ask him as to what were the orders for me. He said the brigade commander was very happy with my work and he had one more task for me. I was supposed to meet the brigade commander on the 18th of January and then he would brief me about my next task.

I was not sure weather it was really some task or was there a displeasure waiting for me for having toppled the Gypsy. Anyway I had to go and see.

The next morning I went to the Brigade headquarters and met the Brigade Commander. He said that 26 January was around the corner and they were expecting some trouble from the militants. There was one particular area which was about 100 kilometers from the Brigade Headquarters and he wanted me to be effective over there on 21st of January. He told me to take the further details from the Brigade Major. The Brigade Major's instructions were snappy. First of all my company was to be attached with a company of the another battalion which was located about 25 kilometers from the place where I was to be deployed. Second, there were no telephone lines in the area so I should carry one radio set with booster so that I could communicate with the Brigade Headquarters and the battalion when required. Third was there was no medical cover available to me so I had to carry two nursing assistants with me. The fourth was that my company was supposed to be self contained with rations for eight days.

 I rushed out of the Brigade Major's office and called up our adjutant and conveyed all these requirements to him. He agreed to send me the required manpower and material. Rations I was supposed to draw from the Brigade supply point. I immediately went to the supply point and placed indents for eight days rations and 300 kilometers of fuel, oil and lubricants for the vehicles and for the cookhouse. In the meantime I conveyed the orders to my company senior JCO so that he could make the necessary preparations. We de-inducted to the Brigade Headquarters on 19 January and moved for the new location in Assam at 0700 hrs on 20 January. We went as per the standard operating procedures for convoy movement, being peculiar about the vehicle to vehicle distance, speed limit and the two hour breaks and reached the new location at 1230 hours. I was supposed to meet the 'gaon budha' of that village and ask for accommodation. He told me that there were only four rooms available in the school which was closed till 26th of Jan. We opened the school, set up the benches to one side and accommodated our self. While this setting was on I opened the radio set and informed the CO that all was well and we will take care of the situation. In the meantime my troops had set up an adhoc langhar (cookhouse) at the compound wall of the school and we had hot meals.

In the evening I went out to see the area from the point of patrolling and domination. I found that the area was vast and the roads were narrow. Patrolling the entire area on foot was not possible and we had heavy vehicles which could not be taken in the depth areas. I decided to decrease the mobility of the locals and increase our own mobility. We borrowed 10 bicycles from the village for five days and patrolled the area with bicycle mounted patrols. We returned the bicycles to the owners on the 27th of January and compensated the owners with some remuneration as rent.

In the meantime I had established communication with the neighboring company commander, and we had started getting fresh rations from him. I was expecting to de-induct on 27th of January but I was informed by our Adjutant that we were to continue in that location till the 12 th of February ie almost two weeks more. Now the school had to be vacated and I shifted the company to the community hall. Resources are secondary and the show must go on. Thereafter we continued with foot patrolling. On 29 Jan I got a call from the neighboring company commander who told me that we were to carry out a joint operation in the Kilo forest. Kilo forest was located in between my company location and his company location On the map it covered five km by five kilometers. He said that he would establish stops on the other side of the forest and I should search through the forest and link up with them.

I told him that I would get 15 persons in the search and destroy patrol and he should put stops with 40 persons to which he agreed.

I started the search about 9 am in the morning. I knew that I had to move from west to the east and the sun would be on my face. We started in extended line but in a short while we were in a single file. Once we entered inside the forest there was no sunlight. There was bamboo forest with dense undergrowth at some places. We marched for about two hours and reached a place where the soil was moist. Soon we were in knee deep water and sweating profusely. We had lost all sense of direction, dodging the dense undergrowth and at one point we were lost. All 15 of us were to-gather and lost. We had not anticipated this and we were not carrying a magnetic compass either. The only thing missing was the Bengal Tiger.

I even asked the troops if anyone had a needle so that we could use it like a compass. Just then one of the jawans came out with a keychain which had a floating magnetic globe with north marked on it. It worked like a compass. It took us four hours to cross 5 km of forest and we linked up with the stops at around 1 pm.

Training the Recruits to Norhona Banner

I was posted to the Regimental Centre as a Training company commander. I reported to the Centre and I was given charge of the Seramany company, which was located on the Ava Hill Complex. Apart from being away from the main Barracks there were some command and control problems with the company. There was history of one weapon having been stolen from the company kote which was later found and placed back. The company had been coming last in all the intercompany events.

On the very first day I came to know that the Inter company football match was to commence after four days, and I already had one football medal in my Kitty. That same day I told them to layout their dress, shoes and socks and sanctioned funds to purchase new dress and equipment. The very next day the new dress was ready. In the meantime I included the reserve players in the team and made two practice teams. One team would play the practice match in our ground while one team would go and play at the main barracks. The boys were told to observe the players of the other teams. After the games parade we would get togather and discuss the games played.

Our effort worked and we won the finals. There was an immediate change in the outlook of the company. Immidiately after the final match on the same evening we had the company badakhana to facilitate the players and at the same time the voulenteers for the next intercompany sports event, which was volleyball, were taken. This good stead continued and we won the finals of seven out of the ten intercompany events in the training year. The Company was awarded the Norrona banner.

Post Tsunami Relief Operations

My book would be incomplete if I do not write about the Post Tsunami relief operations. I was posted in Wellington at the Regimental Center as the training company commander. I had gone on leave to Mumbai and my leave was to terminate on the 25th of December. But I had decided to come back to Wellington on the 23rd of December, to look after my personal adm before joining back. On 24 Dec at about noon I got a call from the training battalion commander. A Tsunami had struck the eastern coast of India and it had left the area devastated. Our Regimental Center was tasked to send two columns to Cuddalore district which was severely affected. I was the column commander for one of the columns.

We had to mobilise from Wellington within six hours. That meant we had to move out of our barracks by 6 pm and then travel through the night and then reach Cuddalore by morning. Out Deputy Commandant was moving with us as the overall contingent commander. He briefed us that for being effective we had to reach intact. Again I was tasked to lead the convoy. I would have been keen to move the convoy at sixty kilometers per hour, but the Deputy Commandant had personally briefed the driver that if he exceeded 40 kmph or allowed me to drive, he would be marched up and punished the very next day. And this warning was given in my presence.

We reached Cuddalore at about 6 am next morning. The District Collectors office was next to the police station. Some distance from the police station was an open shed which might other wise have been a parking lot. There were about 20 bodies lying over there all tied up in white cloth.

The District Collector came in a short while. My column was tasked to go to Parangipettai, which was about 30 kilometers from Cuddalore. I took my column to Parangipettai at around 10 am and met the Sub collector over there. We were housed in two rooms in a school building. We had carried our personal weapons over there, but the personal weapons were not required over there as we were required to rescue and relief operations. Structures were damaged upto a hundred meters from the shoreline, more in some low lying areas. There was debris lying around and there were people and amimals trapped under the debris. On the first day we rescued five dead bodies, from under the debris. There was so much stench of rotting flesh in the area that we could not have any food after coming back. People were sitting under their fallen houses with blank faces.

In the meantime truckloads of relief materials had started moving into the area with clothes medicines and food. This was serious business and things had to be organized. The problem was with cooked food which was cooked two days back in Bangalore and sent here as some items had gone sour. There was stagnant water and mosquitoes, add cholera and we could have an epidemic.

In the evening I went to the sub-collectors office. I told him that I wanted him to pass some orders to the villagers on the loudspeakers. First of all all villagers should clean their houses and keep the dirt and debris out side the houses. Second I wanted the volunteers for each locality to collect this dirt and dump it at the end of the road for the municipal staff to collect it. Third I wanted to see a pot of rice boiling in every house. As for the aid coming from Bangalore was concerned we set up a joint check post at the entry of the village to check the aid before allowing it into the area. We were able to contain the situation and our columns were de-inducted after ten days.

Notes :

In disaster relief, the most important function is to raise the morale of the affected population. Making them cook their own food is the easiest method to instill high morale.

The next important task is to get rid of clutter. Cleaning of the houses and neighboring locality was carried out to that effect.

After a disaster the casualties are more due to spread of diseases. That has to be controlled.

A Bouquet Full of Thorns

This was one year in which I had the ultimate taste of soldiering. I was posted in an area which was in highly infested with terrorists. So much so they had almost declared it independent of the Indian government. There were three mountain ridges in our area of responsibility. It was known to be having 16 – 17 militants and locals said that they moved in groups of four to five at night. I had been posted in this area in Nov and I had to undergo pre-induction training at the corps battle school for almost 40 – 45 days before getting inducted in the operational area. I had about 10 days in the unit rear which was not far from the op area. It was just the third day that I had taken over as the second in command of the unit when one militant came on to my radio frequency and started telling me, " Aap naye aye ho to niche hi rehna, upar aa gaye to wapas jana mushkil hoga (You are new, so better you say down. If you come up , it wil be difficult to go back)." That was too much arrogance. I switched off my radio set and told our signal operator to shift to reserve frequency.

I came back from the corps battle school and was inducted into the op area. I visited all the posts and then I was to stay at Romeo Juliet post. Romeo Juliet was a platoon post of the bravo company. It looked directly into the valley between Bravo company and Delta company. There was no electricity at this post and there was only one 3 KVA generator set which was used for charging of the radio set batteries and HHTI batteries. HHTI was 'Hand Held Thermal Imager'. It was an instrument which I was using for the first time and I liked the most. I would sit with it after dinner and observe the area. The snow in the lower parts of the valley had started melting and there was dense forest in many places. I could see the movement of some persons at night in groups of 4 to 5 and I was sure these were the same militants. I discussed these with my company commanders. I was convinced that there was a lot of scope for good operations to be carried out. I patrolled the areas to see from close but during the day everything seemed normal.

It was just about two days after that there was some input about two militants hiding in some village. The commanding officer was in charge of the operations. I too had joined the cordon with my team. When I reached the location I immediately recognized the hut as a hideout. The cordon was laid and I had taken up position bang opposite the entrance to the hideout. I was at a higher level and a burst from my weapon would have been lethal to any terrorist coming out of the hideout. The automatic grenade launcher was located to my far left at right angles to the hideout. One grenade was fired from the grenade launcher. The grenade burst on the top of the hide out and one splinter flew in my direction. This splinter hit upon my elbow, but I did not feel much pain. Just then the jawan on to my left turned on to his side and said, " Sir aap ke hath se to khoon a raha hai. I turned to my side and saw that there was blood dripping from my elbow. I had pulled myself behind. Just then the terrorist who was hiding inside the hideout rushed out firing indiscriminately with the AK 47 in our direction. Since we had pulled back he did not get us. Not withstanding the militant escaped.

On one of my morning patrols I went to a dhok where some people were staying. I went there and sat on a tree stump, when one of the locals came up to me and requested me not to sit on that stump. He requested me to come and sit on a chair on the other side of the dhok. Later on after a few months this dhok happened to be destroyed as a militant hideout and we had an encounter with militants over there.

On another instance I was on a patrol moving up from the valley towards my post when I suddenly encountered a man who was stockily built and had a very well manicured thick beard. He had the complete body language of a militant but he was not carrying a weapon on him.

He had one identity card of some institution in the neighboring district. While I was talking to him I saw one person moving on the neighboring spur, which was about two hundred meters from the spur in which we were climbing halting near a tree and looking at us. We frisked the person who was near us and let him go. This was the great dichotomy of counter insurgency operations. We could not arrest a person without evidence of his being involved in insurgent/terrorist activity and we could not open fire unless we were fired upon. The next morning I went on a patrol to visit Echo company commander at his company post. En-route we came upon a village where we came across a scraggy looking man who ran upon seeing us, and bumped into one of my scouts who was moving from the upper side of the village. Again he said he was running after the goats and we had to leave him, much to our discomfort.

I went to the bravo company and the company commander welcomed me to the company post. Just as I was entering inside I noticed the sentry at the gate was very smartly dressed. The pouches on his chest were square and not sagging. I remarked to him, "smart pouches" and at the same time shook the pouch with one hand. They seemed to be very light. I told him to remove the magazine he was carrying and to my surprise it was an empty magazine. I told him to remove all the magazines he was carrying and they were all empty. The company commander was embarrassed and I told him to take care of such tendencies among the troops.

I had lunch with him and we discussed the various movements I had seen from the HHTI. Just two days after that I de-inducted to the battalion rear location where I was supposed to look into the administration of the troops as second in command of the unit.

The First Encounter

The militant moment in the three ridges was more than we could be comfortable with. Even the company commanders were convinced that we had to do something to tackle the militants. This was especially because they were all trained across the border and infiltrated and settled into our area. The first to pick up was the company commander of Echo company. He took evening patrols to the forest in the re-entrant opposite the Romeo Juliet. Then on the fourth day he took a large patrol of about seventeen jawans. Twelve of them returned back while he along with five jawans stayed back in an ambush. As appreciated by him they had an encounter at around midnight and one militant was killed and one AK 47 recovered. The dangerous game had just begun. Shortly the commanding officer proceded on leave and I was the officiating commanding officer.

The next to take on was the Foxtort company commander. The foxtort company was located on the ridge opposite the Echo company. The Echo company had killed a militant on the Foxtort company ridge and now Foxtort company was seeing movement on the Echo company ridge. He had been observing movement from a house next to the dhok where I had been sitting and a local had requested me to shift myself a few days back. Bravo company was also located on the same ridge so the operation was launched in conjunction with Bravo company. They had laid cordon to the place and then they were planning to search the area when one grenade was lobbed by the militant from inside the house. The house had a flat roof and one door and two windows on either side. Our troops jumped to the side and the grenade rolled down the hill before it blasted. They cordoned off the area and a fire fight ensued.

I was at the Tactical headquarters of the battalion which was co-located along with the Alpha Company. At this time I had started from the Tactical headquarters but I had to cross two valleys and one ridge of Foxtort Company before getting to the encounter site. In the meantime I was informed that one of our Jawans was injured due to an AGL(Automatic Grenade Launcher) round and the firing was still on.

I had to reach the location before I could say anything. The adjutant was a young officer with just six years of service and he inadvertently reported to the Brigade Headquarters that one Jawan had got injured in practice firing of AGL. The GOC wanted to know what was happening and he came on to the radio set to speak with me. I was just climbing down the second valley and it would take me around 40 minutes more to reach the encounter site. I informed the GOC that we had one casualty and needed a helicopter for casualty evacuation, and that I would get back with the further details. When I reached the encounter site we had two militants dead and one soldier injured due to gunshot wound in the head. The bullet had skirted the helmet and got into his head. He was evacuated by helicopter. I conveyed the report to the Brigade Headquarters and the GOC on radio. We carried out the punchanama with the police and I walked back to the Tactical Headquarters.

Chance Encounter of the Road Opening Party

The commanding officer was on leave in his hometown, but the adjutant had been updating him on the operations on the phone. Now the ridge on which the Echo and the Bravo company were located, over-looked the National highway on the other side. The Bravo company was tasked to send a Road Opening party from the Northern side. Now the adjutant in consultation with the CO decided that since Bravo company was involved in the operation the previous day, the road Opening Party should go from the Echo company.

The next day was Sunday, but the convoy was moving. The road opening party started from the Echo company op base. There was a local dog at the Echo company op base and the dog moved with the Road opening party. They had moved about a kilometer from the company op base, when suddenly the dog barked towards the front and there was a burst of Ak 47 fire which came on to the troops.

 Now it so happened that the 'Road Opening Party' had moved from a different direction so the militants had not got intimation from their informers. There were in fact three militants who were sitting over here and having food when the dog barked and they got startled and let out a burst on our troops. The leading scout returned fire and went to the ground. We had no injuries but the scout informed that one of the militants had been hit. The militants had run towards the left side of the ridge.

The company commander at Echo company was informed by his troops that they had come under fire. He immediately got ready and moved out of his post with his quick reaction team. When the company commander reached the location he asked the road opening party as to which direction the injured militant fled. Immediately the company commanders scout started moving in that direction. The scout had just marched about 10 meters when there was a single shot fired and the scout fell flat on his face. The company commander who was moving close behind called out the name of the scout and bent over him to pick him up. Just then one more shot was fired and the company commander got a bullet and fell down.

It had so happened that while the two militants had fled the injured militant had not been able to run far and had hid himself behind a fallen tree. He had taken up position such that he got the scout in the first shot and the company commander in the second shot. Both the company commander and the scout were airlifted but could not be saved. The injured terrorist was eliminated in retaliatory fire.

Operations Continued

The next operation was again in the area of Romeo Juliet. This was again a joint operation by Foxtort and Bravo company. The bravo company commander gave me a call on the radio set at 2 am in the night. My radio set was always on and it was right next to me. He informed me that some movement had been observed by the Echo company commander and also by his own night patrol over the HHTI and they were moving in for the cordon. I gave him the go ahead to lay the cordon and told him that I would join the operation later. I started at 7 am and reached the Bravo company location by 8.30 am. Immidiately on reaching there I started to move towards Romeo Juliet side. I had just crossed the first knoll when I heard the sound of one explosion followed by two bursts of AK 47.

 Now while the cordon had been laid and the Bravo company commander was moving towards the suspect house a grenade was lobbed from the suspect house. The company commander and his scout dashed to the ground and the grenade rolled down hill and burst. Own troops fired two bursts and took position on the ground. I continued to move towards the encounter site. In the meantime we heard two bursts of gunfire fired from the jungle below us and this time we also heard the puttering of bullets going overhead. I was very sure someone was firing upon us and his bullets were going over our heads. We continued to move ahead to get out of a possible ambush and moved to the main encounter site.

 After reaching the site I took up position next to the Foxtort company commander. As I sat there on scraggily dressed man came out of the window of the house and started looking around. I could not see any weapon in his hand and it was difficult to decide to fire upon him. I turned my weapon to fire upon him but the F company commander shouted, sir no, our troops are ahead. Just one split second and this man went leaps and bounds and ran down the hill. On the way he dropped one magazine and we realized that he was carrying a weapon as well. He vanished before we could react. There was another burst fired from inside the house. but we brought down fire on the house and kept the house pinned. We were sure there were more terrorists in the house. In the meantime the Echo company commander had prepared two explosives to blow up the suspect house. Just as the explosives got ready the militants inside the house started firing again. We made the explosives and placed them one after another on the roof of the house and blasted them . The roof came down and the firing from inside stopped.

Removing the debris and searching the house was again a risky operation. We had no idea of the type of underground hideout inside the house. If the militant were alive, they could fire upon our troops when we opened the debris. I ordered that we keep the cordon for four more hours and then enter the house. Two militants were killed in the encounter while two AK 47s and one Pika Gun were recovered from the house.

 We made the recoveries, conducted the panchanama with the local police and handed over the slain militants for their further cremation. It was last light by this time. Just then one militant came on the radio set on my frequency and spoke, " Bade militant marta hai. Jara apna patka utar , dekh kaise headshot leta hun (Killing militants, eh, Just remove your patka and see how I take a head shot)". This transmission was heard by the troops around me and they told me to sit down and took up positions around me. I was supposed to move out from there but I decided to hold on over there for the night. There was no further transmission on my radio set.

The next day we marched back to the Bravo company location in the morning. In a short while the Brigade Commander arrived over there to congratulate us.

The third Militant who had run down the hill was a self styled area commander of one of the terrorist outfits, and the Div HQ signal regiment had recorded a two page long intercept of him telling his story as to how he had narrowly escaped on that day.

Mopping up of the Terrorists

Later during the year four terrorists were eliminated on the ridge opposite the Tactical Headquarters and two more in the intervening opportunities. As luck would have it I was present in most of the operations. But I always moved around with my bulletproof patka and Jacket.

On one cold night, the company commander at bravo company called me on the telephone at 4.30 am. He said that he had been seeing some movement in the village which was in the valley across his post. It was a small area comprising of three isolated houses. I told him to lay the cordon, and that I will reach shortly.

During the year most of the militants had been eliminated, but there was one name which remained on the dashboard. He was supposed to be a militant of some hierarchy. Mainly because he had been in the area for a very long time. He had been operating in the area below Bravo company where today's cordon had been laid. I had to move by road to Bravo company and then on foot. I reached the Bravo company HQ by 8.00 am and walked down to the cordoned area by 8.30. I then told the company commander to start the search. The company commander's team searched the houses and by ten am he reported that nothing had been found. I told him that I wanted to see the houses myself.

 I with my team entered the first house which was on the farthest side. There was an old couple in the house. The Bravo company troops told me that they had been left in the house because they were old and could not move. The other members of the family were in the other house. The second house was totally empty.

When I came to the third house there was some commotion inside and one lady from the house came and stood in the door of the house. Before I could ask anything she said, "Aurten aur bachhen hai." From the gap on her left I could see one bed on which some ladies and children were sitting. I looked at the lady in the door and she looked straight into my eyes as though begging me not to go inside the house. I immediately stepped to my left, clear of the door and stood near the wall. If there was a militant hiding inside with a weapon pointing towards the door, he could take me down in a single shot and run out. Any firing from me or my troops could cause collateral damage. I decided to call off the operation but I decided to play a psychological trick on the probable militant inside and on the locals. I called the eldest person around and told him in a loud voice, " Aap jante hain ke hamne kitne militant mare hain. Hamari khabar kabhi galat nahi hoti. Hamne iske liye pachhis hazar to advance diye hai. Mujhe pata hai ke voh yahi kahi hai, lekin aaj uski takdeer tavajju par hai. Is liye ham wapas ja rahe hai." I had spoken loud and clear for everyone to hear.

Thereafter I told the B company commander to make a tactical withdrawal and we moved back to the Bravo company. I went back to the battalion rear.

This militant had been enjoying at the cost of the villagers. He would not hesitate in demanding a woman from the village. There was one woman in particular to whom he would go when her husband was out and enjoy himself. At this particular time her husband had just come back from the city and he was carrying eight to ten thousand rupees with him.

On 13 Dec, there was an operational conference at one of the brigade headquarters where about 20 commanding officers had come.   I was officiating as Commanding officer at that time and I also attended that conference. During the lunch I was seated on a table where both my GOC and Brigade Commander were seated. Our unit had performed very well during the year. During the lunch the GOC asked me casually, " So Parag, when is the next kill. I was taken by surprise, but the recent episode with Bravo company was at the back of my mind. I said that we will get one militant within the next two days. Even my Brigade commander was surprised as I had not discussed any plans with him. I said we have been working on it for the last eight days and that we should get him soon. The GOC and the Brigade commander left after lunch.

Now I felt some pressure for what I had said because there was no concrete plan. I called up he company commanders and told them we had to launch multiple ambushes as well as search and destroy missions tonight as there were confirmed intelligence reports from the GOC about this militant moving around in the area and that I would also join them at some point. I called up the battalion rear and told them that I will be moving up to the op location after coming back and they should keep a team ready for that. I moved to the platoon locality of Echo company which was about 20 minutes walk from the road head. My requirements were very minimum in the op areas. I just needed one sleeping bag, two rotis and one large of Old Monk. The company commanders confirmed to me that the ambushes were out . I had put some troops on the HHTI and tucked into my sleeping bag.

Now on this night there were 18 ambushes out in the area and I had moved to the op location. Enough to stir up the area. Message must have gone to the militants. I continued to stay at the op location and repeated the ambushes the next night. I got a call from the Bravo company commander at around 2 am. He said two shots had been fired in the village. Thereafter one villager had come to the company post and said that militants had come to the village and that they required our help. While the company commander was speaking to me two more shots were fired in the village.

I told the company commander to move to the village, and myself too started from the other side. The company commander reached the site of the village after about half an hour. I was still on the way. The company commander informed me on the radio that the militant whom we were targeting had been killed. I reached the site in the village and found that this militant had been killed in the house of the same lady whom he was after. His head had been hit with an Axe, which was lying there itself and he had two bullet wounds in his chest. His AK 47 was kept at the side. I was told that he had come to that lady's house and picked up a quarrel with her husband. He was accompanied by his buddy, (another militant) who was standing out side the house, as guard or early warning. On that night the lady's brother was also present in the house. During the quarrel he started abusing them and pointed his AK 47 in their direction. The two of them overpowered him, one caught hold of his AK 47 and the other put an Axe in his head. The militant fell down but they had both hatred and fear in them. They picked up his AK 47 and fired two bullets in his chest. The militant who was standing outside the house was shocked to see his friend dead and quickly ran away. There after the villagers gathered and one of them came to inform the company commander. This was also confirmed by the HHTI operator at D company.

When the Bravo company commander reached the location or even when I reached the location the lady was no where to be seen. I called for the police from the rear location to do the Panchanama. At about 6 am I came to know that this lady had also died and her body was in the house two houses down the lane. I went down to see her and found that even she had two bullets in her chest.

I called up the brigade commander and told him that the militant had been eliminated. The other militant had escaped and the villagers were afraid that he would take revenge. By around 10 am some people had put up a protest and were denying the cremation of the militant. There was one group which had moved to give dharna on the National Highway. Luckily the SHO from the neighboring district came to Bravo company location and he pacified the villagers, and also carried out the cremation of both the militant and the lady.

The next day there was a congratulatory from the GOC and the B company commander was sent on leave.

The Perfect Ambush

One militant had escaped but his movement had been picked up by our HHTI operators. He had run towards the jungle of Romeo, which was on to the left of Bravo company post. The new company commander at Bravo company called me after eight days and told me that he had picked up the movement of one militant who was most probably the same militant who had escaped and he wanted to launch operations to apprehend him the same night. I told him that we should wait for some time. Then seeing the eagerness of the officer I agreed to come to his post and discuss the matter with him.

The next morning I drove up to the Bravo company and met the company commander. We put two chairs on the top of the company commander's bunker and discussed the plan. I had told him that I was familiar with the area and that there was no requirement of any Indication of landmarks.

This militant's movement had become very predictable. At around 10.30 in the night, one person would start from a particular house in the village and go towards the forest of Romeo. At around 12 am, midnight, two persons would return from the Romeo Jungle and move back into the house. Then at 3.30 two persons would emerge from the house and move back to the Romeo Jungle. At around 4.30, one person would move back from the Jungle to the house.

This meant that he was staying at some hideout in the Romeo forest. One Villager who was helping him would go to the forest and guide him to his house where he would return back by midnight. There he had hot meals, took some rest and then at 3.30 started back for the forest. The villager escorted him to the edge of the forest and then returned back while the militant moved ahead to his hideout.

The Romeo Jungle was on a spur which climbed up on to the ridgeline. About half way up the spur was a patch where the trees were a little sparse. I told the company commander that this was the ideal location to lay the ambush, and that he should try and see with the HHTI whether this militant crossed that patch every night. My second instruction was that on the night of the operation he should send one Ambush in the direction opposite to Romeo at 9.00 pm. This ambush should carry an HHTI and act as an OP for the main ambush. The main ambush should start from the post after 12.30 am, once the militant was comfortably tucked inside the house. The main ambush party should be in location before he started back from the village, and they should also carry an HHTI. I had told him to wait till 31st before launching the ambush. Our Brigade commander proceded on posting on the 30th of the month. The new Brigade commander had called for a conference on the 30th. After the conference we had lunch and I was seated on the same table as the new Brigade commander. He asked me the same question , " so Parag, when is the next kill?" and I gave the same answer, " Two days sir." He asked me who is it this time and I told him the name.

On the 31st I was at the Tactical HQ. We had a small celebration with the troops and I tucked into my bed at 12.30am. At about 4.30 am my buddy woke me up telling me that there was firing towards Bravo company. From the Tactical HQ we could see only flashes as it was far and across one ridge. I knew it was the Bravo Company Commander's ambush. I got my team ready and started for Bravo company location on foot. The ambush party had continued to fire for quite some time. I reached the bravo company location at around 8.30 am. Shortly they brought the mortal remains of the slain militant and the police came and we did the panchanama.

It had so happened that the militant had fired on the ambush party on being challenged and was down in the first retaliatory burst. But his tiffin contained hot meals and that continued to glow for quite some time in the HHTI. Our boys knew how we had lost our Troops and also an officer to militant fire earlier and they continued to fire till the tiffin got cold. The tiffin had about 10 holes in it.

The Sixteen Day Patrol

This was the time when I was posted I the northeastern part of the country. There was a patrol on which I had gone and which was a sixteen day patrol. We were about eighteen persons who were to go on the patrol. I can say that not many people get an opportunity to go on this patrol.

We were airlifted and dropped at a forward village where there was a helipad. We were carrying rations for sixteen days. Of course we were authorized porters to carry the rations with us. The villagers were very hospitable. They had organized a reception for welcoming us and in the evening they also gave a grand party.

On the first day we were to go down the hill upto the river. There was dense forest and the track was steep at places. We started marching at 8am in the morning and by around 12.30 pm we reached the river. After reaching the river we were required to cross the river. The river was more than 100 metres wide and the crossing was with the help of a Tawa Bridge. The Tawa Bridge comprised of a single steel wire rope, slung across the river and anchored into the ground in steel and concrete. The crossing aid was a Tawa which was a wooden hangar with

Parachute Straps tied into it. One of the porters demonstrated it to us and went across the bridge unaided. When he went across, he carried one end of the Nylon rope, which was later used to pull the others across when needed. I was very excited to cross the Tawa bridge. For one I was seeing it for the first time, and second it was a real life adventure in operational area. I declared that I will be the first to cross after the porter. The total expanse of the steel wire must have been about a hundred and twenty meters, and there was about hundred meter wide roaring river flowing underneath.

When I got under the steel wire and tied the parachute rope around me. It took me across for the first sixty to seventy meters on gravity. During this time I had to keep my hands on the wooden block of the Tawa, so that my hands don't get cut. There was a safety rope tied to my waist, so that the porter in front could pull me after crossing the first 70 meters. It took about forty minutes for all of us to cross the river. After crossing the river we looked for a camping site and set up our bivouacs. The boys made sambhar and rice and we had a sumptuous meal. In the afternoon some of us went to have a bath in the small pool that was formed next to the river. By evening our porters managed to catch some fresh fish from the river and we had a nice dinner.

The next day we woke up at 4.30 am. In the east the sun rises early. Early morning we were visited by two huge mithuns (bisons). They came when most of us were on our shallow trench latrines. Any how we wound up our business and closed the camp and we started for our next location.

Our patrol instructions read that the area ahead was infested with blood sucking leaches and we all had to carry salt tied in kerchiefs to tackle the leaches that managed to get on to our skin. In fact in one of the patrols two persons had to be evacuated by helicopter, because they were attacked by more than a hundred leaches. Any way we all were safe.

The track ahead was no game. It started with a gentle slope in tall grass and undergrowth. The leading porters had to cut our way through with their sharp dahs. We kept climbing for an hour and then walked on an undulating mountain side for about two hours. After that we had to cimb down a steep slope. There were huge trees on this slope, some of them perhaps more than hundred plus years old, and we had to climb down holding on to the matted roots of those trees.

We climbed down towards the river bed and then the path was literally through the river bed in which there were huge round stone boulders. We had to jump from boulder to boulder and I felt like a monk from the thirty six chambers of shaolin.

We reached the second day camp site and settled down for the day. We continued the same routine day after day. The porters moving with us were very resourceful and they hunted wild foul on one day and wild goat on another day.

I had visited some local houses before starting on the patrol and had seen that they had a very nice way of preserving meat. They had a fireplace in the center of the house where they cooked their meals, and they had loafs of meet suspended from the ceiling, so that they were about four feet from the fire. The meat dehydrated by the heat of the fire. They would scrape out some meat before their cooking and use it in their meals.

 Our patrol continued and by day four we had reached a higher altitude and the leaches had subsided. On day six we reached the tributary of a river which we had to cross with the help of a log bridge. This bridge was just a single log fitted on to wooden spikes. There were two logs in succession and they were water washed and slippery with no support on top. Anyway we crossed them. On day seven we reached a lace which was totally marshy. There was no place to camp. So we jumped the halt and reached the place where we were supposed to go on the eighth day and camped there.

We stayed there till day eight. We absorbed the full spectrum of nature from there. Cold wind, rain, mist, fog, harsh sunlight and a very very starry sky at night. All in a single day.

We were carrying three banners all written in Chinese language. The first read, " This is our land, you please go back." The second read, "This is our land, you please go back. We will also go back." The third read, " This is our land. Since you are not going back, we will go back and report to our government." Luckily the Chinese patrol didn't come and we did not use the banners.

On day nine we started our way back. The way back was comparatively easy as it was all down slope. Only the weather had gone crazy as it was overcast and raining every day. Finding dry wood, lighting a fire and cooking food was an issue.

On day sixteen we crossed the Tawa bridge and climbed up to the village where there was a helipad and from where we had started. We were authorized a two night halt at the village, to close the accounts and pack our stores. On the third day we were supposed to be airlifted by a chetak helicopter but the weather was totally packed up and we were told we had to march back on foot for another two days to reach our unit. We had left two boys with the heavy stores to be airlifted when the weather improves. We started on foot and on the next day the weather improved. Our boys with the stores were airlifted and they reached before we could reach the unit.